In friendship and love,

To _____

From _____

©CARLTON CARDS, CLEVELAND, OH MADE IN U.S.A.

ISBN 1-56218-007-X

For a Very Special Friend

Designed by Dan Chrzanowski

So many times,
I think of you
throughout
the busy day,
and remember
all the good times
we've had together.
So many times,
I appreciate
what it means
to have a wonderful friend
like you...

...and this is one
of those times!

Sometimes you meet someone
you feel will be a lifelong friend.
That's how I felt when I met you.
Since then, our friendship
  has grown and gotten better...

We've learned to trust each other,
support each other,
depend on each other—
and open ourselves up
to show each other
the part of ourselves
we don't often let the world see.
If friends like us
can tell each other anything,
I want to tell you
you're the closest
and most wonderful friend
that I have ever had.

Remembering You

Thinking of you
and remembering the good times
and the sad times we've shared
with our own
special kind of closeness.
Thinking of you
and feeling especially blessed
to have you to turn to
and count on
and remember
with such happiness.
You're some kind of friend!

Thank You for Being My Friend

Thank you for being so generous
with your own very special gifts
of thoughtfulness and caring,
loving and laughter, serenity and joyfulness.

Thank you for being so generous
with the very special gift
of yourself!

You're
Always There
When
I Need You

You're always there
when I need you.
Whenever I need someone to talk to,
you're always there
to listen and share your point of view.
Whenever I need a favor,
you're always there
to help out any way that you can...

Whenever I need encouragement
or I'm feeling down,
you're always there
to lend moral support
and give my spirits a lift.
No matter what
or when or where or why,
you're always there
when I need you.

I hope you know
how much I value
your caring and friendship—
how much I admire
the generous, giving person
you are.

As long as there are people who care,
the world is still a place
of possibility and hope.
As long as there are people
who reach out and give,
each day still holds
a wealth of special moments.
As long as there are friends like you,
my life is filled
with the greatest joy—
the joy of knowing someone
who is caring and kind,
who reaches out
in warmth and honesty
and understanding.

Because You're My Friend

If I've become
a kinder, better person,
it's because I've known you.
If I've learned to appreciate
life a little more,
it's because you've shown me
how to enjoy being alive
and to take each day as it comes.
If my world seems happier,
the future brighter,
it's because of you—
because you're my friend.

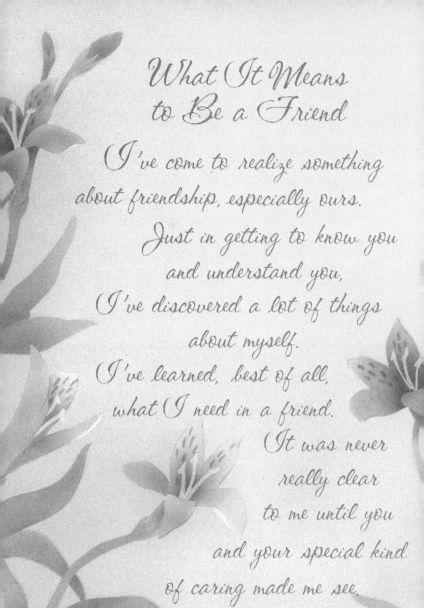

What It Means to Be a Friend

I've come to realize something
about friendship, especially ours.
Just in getting to know you
and understand you,
I've discovered a lot of things
about myself.
I've learned, best of all,
what I need in a friend.
It was never
really clear
to me until you
and your special kind
of caring made me see.

Isn't it funny how we can go along
enjoying the laughter and sharing
that friendship holds,
not realizing how much
we're learning about ourselves
from each other?
I never thought
of that before,
but then I've never had
a friend like you before.
You are very special.

Oh, the comfort
of feeling safe with a person,
having neither to weigh thoughts
nor measure words,
but pouring them all right out,
just as they are,
chaff and grain together;
certain that a faithful hand
will take and sift them,
keep what is worth keeping,
and then with the breath of kindness
blow the rest away.

A Friend
Takes the Time to Help

There have been times
when you didn't have any time,
and yet, you took the time.
There have been times
when you had enough cares
of your own,
and yet, you cared.
There have been times
when you had given
all you had to give,
and yet, you kept on giving.

Thank you.

The Language of Friendship

In friendship,
there's a language
that we understand
only with the heart.
Maybe that's why
we seem to take
good and faithful friends
for granted...
the words of gratitude
are spoken
by one heart to another.

But sometimes, still,
    it's good to say
        in so many words
how you've made my world
    a little warmer...
        a little brighter...
little friendlier!

Your Special Ways

You have a way of putting
others first,
without even trying!
You have a way
of looking straight
at a situation and seeing it
as no one else sees it.
You have a way
of helping out
before anyone
even asks...

In fact, you have
so many different ways
of being special—
of being you—
that I can't count them all
or name them all!

Stay just the way you are!

Friends

Whenever I have a secret
that just has to be shared,
I remember how lucky I am
to have a friend
as wonderful as you are,
because I can tell you anything
and never need to worry
whether my secret will go further,
and never need to wonder
if you'll be judging me...

There's probably only one thing
I appreciate more
than being able to trust you
so completely,
and that is
knowing you trust me
in just the same way.

I'm so glad we're friends.